HERE.

HERE.

LINDSEY KUGLER

This book published by University of Hell Press.
www.universityofhellpress.com

Book Design & Cover by Vince Norris
www.norrisportfolio.com

Photographs by the author.

Published in the United States of America.
ISBN 978-1-938753-03-9

Sally has a problem. Sally is a music slut. She plays with everyone. She has two regular bands, and some sidemen she jams with. When parties get late and loud, she will pull out her instrument and play with people she just met, people she hardly knows, people whose names she cannot remember—or never knew! She plays for money, she plays for beer, sometimes she even plays just to get an audience, because she likes the attention.

—THOMAS MACAULAY MILLER
"Toward a Performance Model of Sex"

DO YOU?

Do you want me to take you to work? Do you want me to make you food? Do you want me to wash your work clothes? Do you want me to rub your head? Do you want to watch a movie? Do you want to get a tattoo? Do you want me to take you to the shop? Do you want me to take you to your friend's house? Do you want to get drunk?

FREEDOM.

My father is a truck driver and I have a genetic love of the open road. I decided to leave my parents' house in Tucson, Arizona and drive fifteen hours to Austin, Texas in one shot by myself. Originally my father offered to drive with me and fly back. Then he suggested my older brother go along. I refused each offer; I wanted to get lost. "It's different for a girl," my father said. "I'm nervous about you wandering out there by yourself." But, I knew I could do it and I knew I would love it. On my twenty-second birthday, I put my little dog in my little red car. This was my daring escape from a dead-end desert. A job waited for me in Austin. No money, no clue. During the drive, we stopped at flat rest stops. There were red rock-bedded dog parks and bee-infested trashcans. Every time we stopped at a desolate truck stop there was never anyone else around. West Texas is empty. I then realized: my phone could die, my car could die, and we could die. But we didn't. Fig, my Chihuahua and Schnauzer mix, and I arrived in Austin late in the evening. I was to meet my then-best friend in an apartment she chose for us with none of my help. The first thing I did was beg her for a key to the apartment so I could confront an unshakable urge to meet my then-boyfriend in person.

DAY JOB.

I was a superhero. I worked the nine-to-five sorting through the day-to-day problems of formerly homeless elderly. My official title was "Volunteer." I served my country on a living stipend we calculated to be around four dollars an hour. By night I was a villain.

DISGUISED AMONG THEM.

The other kids in my national service program were around my age. Most of us had moved to Austin from other parts of the country but there were a few smiling locals in the group. We were all wide-eyed and unassuming but they had college degrees. I dropped out of Arizona State University just shy of the end of my junior year. I told everyone it was because the program was deteriorating—which was true—but I have never abandoned a sinking ship. I actually missed class after class that spring due to my inability to stay rooted in reality. I could not stop crying and I could not get out of bed. I couldn't explain it to anyone. It was laziness, my mother supposed. I was privileged, white, and reasonably well taken care of, she argued. When it got to the point that I was thinking about hurting myself there was a professional called to deem it something genetic, something embarrassing. When our national service group had the preliminary time-intensive trainings I realized I was not like the others. We shook hands. We told jokes. We waited for people to tell us what to do.

POSSUM.

Late one night I was sitting on the picnic tables outside of my first apartment in Austin. The complex was squeezed between a used car dealership and a Walgreens. Just south of the complex was an invisible line of privilege. Houses sprung up with lush well-trimmed yards and sprawling safe parks. On that night no one was outside except the one guy who was checking on his laundry every fifteen minutes. I watched him, hunched over on the table. A light breeze pushed through the leaves causing a soft rustling sound behind me. I was talking to an ex-boyfriend on the phone. I saw, crossing the sidewalk and lumbering toward me, a furry creature with a white face. I had never seen anything like it before. Its black beady eyes looked up at me and I stopped talking. "What the fuck is that?" I asked. I stammered and squirmed on the picnic table as the creature approached. Closer and closer it came and I panicked. I wasn't sure if what was coming at me was a sign of rabies and I was even less sure if this creature was naturally ferocious. Finally it lost interest and disappeared in the distant grass. I realized I had stopped paying attention to the phone call and apologized. My ex-boyfriend thought he might have cancer.

LOVE ON SLAUGHTER LANE.

I first met my then-boyfriend in person off Slaughter Lane. The street made me nervous for a lot of reasons. The biggest being the name. He suggested we meet at a corner store so he could buy cigarettes but that made me even more anxious. I decided meeting him on a dark side street was better. My then-boyfriend lived with his ex-brother-in-law who taught him how to blow glass pipes, let him live at his house, and use his studio. Their relationship was often strained by the demands of business and my then-boyfriend's inherent artistic talent with glass. In order to pay rent my then-boyfriend spent a lot of time pulling long strips of colored glass called "stringers." Or he spent hours and hours compiling other complicated pieces of smoking appliances. I liked watching him with his goggles on, melting and moving glass. Some people are true performers without even noticing. He smashed glass with the grace of some weather god—containing a perfect hailstorm in his workspace. We spent most of our time at his ex-brother-in-law's house in three areas: the glass studio, his bedroom, and right out front on the driveway when he took his constant smoke breaks. During those breaks we always ran out of things to talk about. I learned how to suppress everything I wanted to tell him and just stay quiet. Just listen. He didn't always want to talk and we would take the pressure off each other by watching his neighbors. I tried to remember my old ballet moves, pirouetting on the concrete as rain fell on the warm ground. Sometimes I would just stand close to him with my arms folded up to my chest in prayer. I would kiss his cheek or neck while he smoked and it always made him uncomfortable—he moved away and spit through the gap in his front teeth. It made a loud squirting sound I will never forget. I longed to hear that sound. It punctuated jokes, angry words, and I love yous. One time he chased me across the street without moving his feet. He shot spit through his teeth like a super soaker and I squealed. I had only been in love once before and it felt like I was wading through warm Vaseline. I was comfortable, shiny, and well lubricated.

TWO CHAIRS.

It was a normal house with an overgrown backyard. The neighbor's dogs barked at us when I walked up to the front door. She answered the door, asked my name, and then told me to meet her out off the side of the house by the garage. She pulled open the garage door and I saw it was overflowing with boxes stacked on old furniture stacked on other boxes. She was not my client but I was sent to practice talking to her like she was. When I called to set up our meeting she told me I was not allowed to wear perfume or come inside the house. She asked me not to bathe with any scented body wash or use any scented body lotion. That morning I just chose not to bathe at all since all the products I owned had fragrances. She set up two chairs amidst the tall grass, one white plastic with a comforter on it for herself and a wire one with no cushioning on it for me. I sat with the paperwork rustling in my lap; it begged to fly onto the streets from the heavy breeze. "We have to move the chairs," she said. She was downwind of me. After dragging the chairs in a circle I asked her about her life. She couldn't hear me well so she asked me to speak louder. I was not permitted to move my chair closer. Her long, thin blonde hair was pinned on top of her head and she wore a pink bathrobe and slippers. She loved her backyard. She lived alone but her son occasionally visited. Due to her severe allergies no one came over that often and never stayed longer than an hour. I was supposed to ask her about her financial planning and her bookkeeping. She could not find individual receipts even though she kept them all stacked in her garage. They came out of her purse, she told me, and went into various boxes or on tables. Once tucked away they disappeared from her memory. They could have all been little sheets of flash fiction, for when she looked at them she couldn't comprehend having purchased what they said she purchased. She told me she was very tired and that her therapist was on vacation but she would call her every day anyway. I wrote in her file that she was apparently the same as the last time someone visited.

LONELY MOTHERS.

I adopted Fig in college. I left her alone too much in the townhouse I shared with my brother and she began to develop a nasty personality usually reserved for froth-mouthed Dobermans who guarded junkyards in movies. After spending money I didn't have on personal dog training services she was no better behaved. At less than ten pounds she was smart—so much so that she trained everyone to be afraid of her. When we arrived in Austin I was swept up by the new life and my new then-boyfriend. I left her crated for as long as I could but I came to see she needed to be with someone who would pay attention to her. I met a woman deeply west of the city. She had a ranch with marbleized rocks leading up to the front door. Her walls were decorated in photos of other people but no one was around. She told me her husband was an anesthesiologist in Chicago and her two children were away at college. She was alone. I brought Fig over later that night and she wandered around the endless backyard. Fig disappeared in the bushes before hopping out like a gazelle. She ran and ran with some grass stuck to her chin. "I think this is perfect," the woman said watching her. I felt newly emptied. "I think so too," I said. When I tried to leave Fig whined and attempted to walk out the door with me. I already warned the woman about Fig's embedded behavior but it felt important enough to repeat. "We'll go to classes every week," she assured me. "We'll go get microchipped tomorrow. Then a shopping trip to PetSmart!" She thanked me and slipped me a nauseating amount of money. I got into my car at the end of her driveway. I sat there for a few minutes, then turned on the air conditioning and drove home. I felt a sense of relief—not for myself but for a dog that needed and craved affection. I never wanted to own a pet again.

MOOSE.

My new roommate had a decrepit Persian grey cat. He was fifteen years old and named Moses—or Moose—my roommate couldn't decide. He lumbered around like a porcupine. His long hair was matted and my roommate tried to groom him on several occasions. His fur was so thick and ratty she could never shave more than a few lines into it before her electric razor broke. She called them his racing stripes. Moses had an abscess on his face that threatened to overtake his eye. The room I moved into used to be his room. His litter box used to sit right in the middle of the hardwood floor. I moved all of my furniture in and started unpacking. I pulled open my bedroom door to let the room air out. Moses slinked in. I said hello and he disappeared into my closet for a few minutes. Then he left. Two days later I discovered he used my closet as a litter box. I threw away a pair of shit-filled shoes. One night my roommate came home and couldn't find him. She started shouting and clapping underneath furniture. She asked me to look under her bed. "I can't do it. Tell me if he's alive," she said standing by her doorway with her hands on her head. I climbed onto her bed and hunched over the edge to see his body nestled against the wall. "He's breathing," I said. She yelled and climbed onto the bed to see for herself. There were a few other times that happened and my stomach always clenched tight with the suspended moment that Moose could've been dead. He actually died a year later when my then-boyfriend and I had already moved away. My roommate put him in the freezer and eventually buried him underneath the red hammock outside the kitchen window.

DEFINED.

An interactive, free, live webcam community for adults. It features models and amateurs in video-chat rooms with sound.

CHERRYWOOD.

If you walked out our front door, turned left and headed down Lafayette Avenue and from there turned right you would run right into Cherrywood. The coffee shop used to be called Quacks and with a new owner came a new energy with lights strung all around. It boasted a large outside section with picnic tables and hard gravel that felt like noisy quicksand. Tuesday nights had comedy shows with the same coke-sniffing comedians that lived in the same apartment complex together. They were a wonky Boy Scout troupe I dreaded seeing around. The rest of the nights were either empty or spotted with aspiring Austin musicians. White noise. Some mornings, around seven or so, my roommate texted me to see if I was awake. If I happened to be she asked me to come sit with her at Cherrywood. I rolled out of bed, got ready for the day, and walked to the coffee shop. She always sat outside with a pair of sunglasses she once found in the bathroom of a bar. They hid most of her face; her small up-turned nose and mouth a perfect expression of don't give a fuck. She had wild Farrah Fawcett hair that was Texas large and glorious. She wrote in a Rhodia notebook with a beer and a Diet Coke in front of her. We talked and she smoked cigarettes. We complained while I drank coffee and picked at cinnamon rolls.

FAMILIAR RIP.

I had not gotten a Brazilian bikini wax before. When I was in high school my mother felt it was of time-sensitive importance to get my eyebrows professionally waxed and plucked by aestheticians. She would schedule the appointment and take me in. I would lie on leather and hold a broomstick while a heavily made-up woman or man ripped hair out of my follicles. I fell in love with the feeling. In Austin, I called the number on the website and a friendly woman answered. She laughed at some of my jokes and we set an appointment. She recommended that I take Advil before the scheduled time since the pain could be awful. I said goodbye to my then-boyfriend the morning of my waxing. He smiled and told me to wake him up when I got back. He wanted to see. My car was sheltering me from an onslaught of rain as I pulled up to the side parking lot of the business complex. The signs were for meditation studios and design firms. At the very bottom was a bright pink sign with a black pinup silhouette. I shook hands with the girl who greeted me at the door. She had long black hair and loud stiletto boots. Her name was Miche. I went to the bathroom and spent a long time trying to examine and clean myself. This was the first time a girl besides my mother would touch me. I was sweating.

CRITIQUE.

I turned on my camera and recorded myself dancing to Ruth Brown. I tried to strip like I saw girls do on reality shows, glossy movies, and in awkward close spaces at parties. I tried to be sexy and I tried to go slow. It felt familiar yet I was making it all up as I went. I sat down to stop the recording and watch what I did and my skin flushed hot. I was embarrassed and full of harsh words for my digital self. My head filled with heat and pressure. I couldn't watch it anymore so I hid it away in one of the many overflowing folders. I later sold the video for $45.

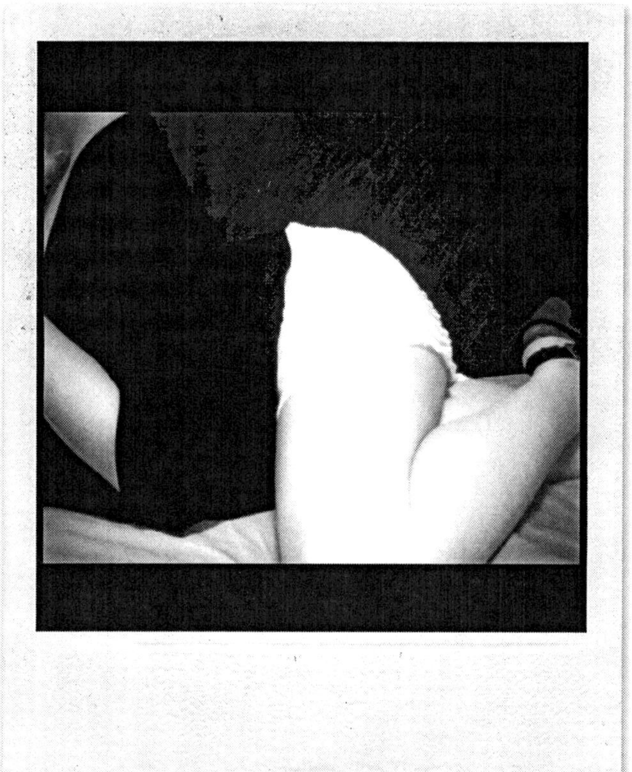

ORNATE FREEDOM.

I pierced my nose right before I went away to Prescott. I was told to let the piercing heal with a glittery stud in it before changing the jewelry but I wanted a silver hoop. I wanted to be Joan Osborne with darker hair. I wore a paisley bikini when we sunbathed in the mountains and by the rivers. We basked like sirens. During the weeks we taught girls aged six to seventeen about self-confidence, achieving goals, and getting through the internal panics. During the weekends we escaped with each other to the small-town bars and unique boutiques. Sometimes we took trips to the less desolate and more tourist-filled spots just to spy on the locals and giggle. We picked through each other's hair, braided it intricately, or cut it all off with exhilarating and often newfound freedom. When we went into town we ate organic things served by trust fund hippies in tiny coffee shops. The girls I grew to love and lived with secluded in the northern Arizona mountains supported me. I wanted to live in the summer forever. On a shopping trip in town we went to the Walmart and pored over the jewelry section. My piercing hadn't healed yet but I couldn't wait any longer. I purchased the hoop and flower set and whined until we drove back to camp. I stood over the sink to get close to the mirror and pushed the stud out of my nose. A rush of pain spiked up through my sinuses.

Pain is weakness leaving the body, I told myself. That was what they said in the Marines, right? Shaking and red, I got the hoop in. I had to take it out shortly after because of the dress code—no noticeable or distracting body modifications were allowed. The piercing became infected but not enough to do anything about it until one night, while on top of my then-boyfriend; I pulled away to see his face smeared with blood and pus. When he noticed the blood his eyes widened and he began to get woozy. He smashed his hand against his face with hysterical force. The nose ring was yanked out amidst our rolling around. I let the wound scar over before getting it pierced again. I still wanted to be Joan Osborne but with a real hoop.

BREAKFAST TACOS & BAGELS.

My then-boyfriend worked two jobs. In the early afternoons he walked down the street to Cherrywood. He made breakfast tacos, burgers, and dishes native to New Orleans—where the owner was from. After frying up food all day he stayed in the kitchen long after the sun set. At night it was rented out to a local wholesale bagel company owned by a former drummer and touring musician. My then-boyfriend spent all night rolling out dough and frying it up with the precise mixture of high gluten and whatever other sticky substances were caked to his beard and arm hair. Then he helped deliver them and came home. For months he did this until he turned into a zombie. Then he did it for a while longer. He slept and worked and the only time I saw him was when he was sleeping. And most times, that was when I was working.

ASSUMPTIONS.

Dorothy was my first client. I spent hours typing up an agenda. I read articles on first-time client meetings and how to create a welcoming and safe space to talk about difficult things like homelessness, abuse recovery, death. I was nervous and sweating. I drove to the apartment complex where we housed several clients. I held a light cream-colored folder to my chest and clomped up the stairs to apartment 137. I knocked on the door and tried to stand up straighter. When Dorothy opened the door I saw she was wearing a red scarf over her hair, a pair of black pants, and a white T-shirt with a faded beer logo on it. She wore a pair of glasses that reminded me of my mother's in old pictures. They ate almost her entire face with a light gold frame and scratched lenses. The skin on her hands stretched to its limit so her knuckles popped up white. She was covered in tiny wrinkles. I introduced myself. We sat on the donated couch facing each other, stiff and erect. I felt stupid. I didn't have any experience in anything and I was expected to fix someone's life. I pulled out the agenda I typed up for us and handed it to her. Dorothy interrupted me. "I can't read this," she said. She looked down at her hands that were constantly picking at each other. I asked if she needed to get her reading glasses but then she told me that she didn't know how to read.

A SEED.

While at a wake, I waited with my mother for her relative-in-law to come around and receive sympathy. My aunt puffed on her cigarette and leaned over to tell me I had a great set of tits and should become a stripper. I didn't know what to say so I said thanks.

DAVID.

David was in love. Nightly he signed on and wrote disjointed staccato poetry. There were lines of misspelled words and stanzas stacked on top of each other about his long days on the road. He drove a rig back and forth across the country. He told me he wrote love letters to the girls who needed them the most. He tried to meet a girl once from the site. Her name was Katrina and he thought she could've been the one. He first sent her a message, and then a picture of his dick, then they spent hours talking on the phone. He loved her a lot and she said she loved him back. I never met Katrina—not even digitally. I saw her perform once where she popped pills and pulled up her shirt. She yelled at the people who requested she show more. She had long dirty blonde hair and wore hot pink. David wrote a part for her in his movie. He was always working on his movie. It was a war story since he was a veteran from Iraq. It ended with him rescuing the girl. He went to high school with someone who was now married to a sitcom writer. This high school friend said she would read his script when he was finished. He told Katrina she would be famous. They agreed to meet on a windy dirt road near where she lived—somewhere in Tennessee. When he pulled up in his truck she was nowhere to be found. He waited for hours but she never showed up.

He called. He begged. He messaged. He got angry. Then he fell in love again but this time it was with me.

COURTNEY.

My then-boyfriend didn't care much for his coworkers—except two of them. One of them was named Courtney. He was a tall, thin, burst of smiling smoothness. He used to tour with a hip-hop group in the early 90s. I always forget the name of it. He was either a DJ, or an MC, or was just around—the story changed depending on whom he was with and when you asked. He was always making a joke, putting his hand on someone's shoulder, or leaning back in a chair. On nights off when the Cherrywood boys played dominoes he wore an eggshell straw hat that was in perfect contrast to his dark, hardened skin. One night I was invited to join them. Courtney talked so fast as he shot the ceramic game pieces across the table. I thought he would make a terrific auctioneer. He called me to join in, "Come on, Ms. Arizona!" But I was too intimidated. Another time he invited me to watch a game of dominoes. I brought my friend Megan. When we walked out to the back deck of Cherrywood he whistled, "Do fries come with that shake?" I didn't bring any more friends around.

SINGING.

My roommate was not home and my then-boyfriend was in the shower. I gave up on doing anything but lying in bed with a pair of ear buds lodged into my ears. I was stomach-down with my feet on the pillows and my head hanging off the foot of the bed. I sang to the floor. My then-boyfriend wandered in and out several times. I suspected he was around but I didn't bother to look up. When I did he was smiling at me while pulling out a cigarette from his pack. Searching for his lighter, he said, "You have a really good, natural voice. You should take some lessons." I smiled and stopped singing.

STAR SEEDS.

The 24-hour diner where my roommate worked the graveyard shift was called Star Seeds. They serve this thing called Rockstar Queso—a liquid cheese dip with guacamole, sour cream, and ground beef mixed in. On nights when my then-boyfriend was not around and I felt myself anxious after midnight I visited my roommate at the diner a lot. If it was a weeknight there wouldn't be very many people in the booths and I always picked the rickety stool along the blue-tiled counter. Sometimes I ate two orders of Rockstar Queso while I watched her spin around, pick up plates and line them up her arms, deliver with smiles, and not write down a single order. She kept everyone's cups filled and chatted artfully. I sometimes went there just to watch her do her job. She made me want to become a waitress but then I remembered in high school I spent one shift in a cheap diner and went home crying. Never again, I reminded myself. But watching her was comforting. Like my then-boyfriend, my roommate smoked as often as she could. She took her smoke breaks out in the front of the diner and I sat with her and watched cars pass on IH 35. Everyone always showed up to Star Seeds expecting more than what anyone who worked there was willing to give. It made me smile, the continuous disappointment of haughty diners. Everyone was pissed about something and everyone who worked there looked tired and worn out the moment they showed up. We all dined in quiet misery and I left with an upset stomach. I climbed into my car and drove home in tears, holding the temptation to hunch over the toilet when I arrived home.

MATURECUNT.

My favorite model on the website's name was MatureCunt. She had a short gray pixie cut and wore bright blue glasses that stayed poised on the edge of her nose like a librarian. MatureCunt was Russian—or at least that's what it noted in her profile, which I wondered if she even wrote herself. She didn't seem to understand or speak any language. She stared at the camera with the kind of glare my grandmother used to give me when I wasn't sitting at the table properly. Her glasses had a glittery chain that wrapped around her ears. I would sit up late at night and watch her. She didn't speak, she didn't play music, and oftentimes she was topless. Just staring at the camera with a silent, naked glare.

SALES TECHNIQUES.

One way I tried to get people to spend more money in my chat room was to pretend to play video games with them off the website. My then-boyfriend was an avid video game player and consented to me giving out his gamer tag to the people who asked for it in my chat room. They would send friend-requests and he would approve them. They would send lurid messages, requests for pictures or videos, and sometimes messages about how great I was at whatever game I was playing. Some of them said they were attracted to me because I played video games well. The truth was that I loved to play the basic games made for children and the times the men thought they were playing first-person shooting games with me they were actually playing them with my then-boyfriend.

JACKSON.

My roommate was in love with Jackson. My then-boyfriend called Jackson "The Vortex of Happiness." Jackson always sat hunched over and mumbled. I never saw him laugh unless it was at someone else's expense. My roommate joked to me about feeling like a battered woman but the truth was that Jackson punched a hole in our wall. She attempted to cover it up with some of her dead father's art so our landlord wouldn't see it. When Jackson was around, my then-boyfriend became tense. My roommate and I found it best to keep them in separate rooms lest we had to break up a fight or call the cops. Jackson pushed my roommate into doors, made her cry, and smashed her guitar.

SHARING.

"Whoa! Finally! A real girl." That, or: "You don't look like you should be on this site. You're like the girl next door." I always looked appreciative of the comments, as if I hadn't thought of that. I sat turned away from the camera, with the right lighting, never with my glasses on unless by request, and always in something vanilla like a white tank top and panties. I wanted to be the girl they spied on through the bedroom window. I discovered that as much as the internet is a safe haven for taboo sex fetishes like water sports, scat, or blood play—it was just as easily a safe space for the sexuality we all thought was ordinary and everyday. A lot of people escaped to the website for simple companionship, emotional discussions, and for me to pretend to be their girlfriend. Some men just liked to look. I liked to be looked at.

STATUE.

When I was little I wanted to become a statue. I loved the story of Medusa and wished she would turn me into stone. I would practice poses waiting for the unforeseen and mythical strike that would freeze me forever. I practiced sexual poses, elegant poses, and goofy poses. I practiced looking in the mirror so I could shift my face from pleasantly present to horrifyingly ugly. It ate me up inside how much I wanted to be stared at.

GHOSTBUSTERS.

There was a big difference between the money I made with my hair straightened versus the money I made when it was left to its naturally curly texture. However, there were some nights I left it wild because some visitors paid more for something different. Jack was one of those visitors. He sent me a message asking me to recreate the scene in *Ghostbusters* where Sigourney Weaver seduces Bill Murray, possessed. He said he would pay for everything—hairstyling, costuming, even furniture. He wanted me to recreate the scene as closely as I could. On top of that he offered to pay me more money than I was ever offered on the website before. I said thanks but turned it down.

SERVICE.

When my then-boyfriend was blowing glass he told me about a time he cut himself seriously. He went to the bathroom to take a leak—having not even noticed the gushing cut on his hand. When he did notice he immediately felt woozy and passed out. His body crashed onto the floor and took a towel rod with him. He came to when his ex-brother-in-law discovered him. He made it very clear to me when we began dating that he would either freak out or pass out if he ever came into contact with blood. When I was menstruating it felt as if I was infected with the most disgusting disease. He stayed away from me. One night I was showering with the intention of trying to get him to sleep with me. I asked and he said if I shaved and showered he would be down. While we were having sex he noticed some blood on him and froze. "What?" I asked, sitting up. He looked pale and started hyperventilating. Now scared, I grabbed onto him. I could tell he was woozy. "What happened?" I asked loudly, trying to get him to respond to me. I helped him sit down, naked, on the bed. It was then I, too, saw the blood and looked down at myself. I cut the inner part of my labia while shaving. "Oh my gosh," I sighed. I got him some water and coached him through his breathing. He didn't pass out but he didn't come near me for a while after that.

HIDING.

The room I rented had a wooden staircase winding up from the backyard along the side of the house to a door that was harder to open every time someone tried. We never used it because it was in direct view of the house behind us and no one was comfortable hanging out on the almost front porch of our neighbors. One night my roommate's friends were in the living room getting ready to go out. Everyone was drinking and my then-boyfriend and I were hiding out in our room. He was playing video games and I was reading. There was a knock on the back door. My then-boyfriend and I exchanged annoyed looks and then helped each other pull open the door. My roommate stood there crying with a lit cigarette. She pleaded with us to come with her or not let her go. She begged me to just let her cry in our room while no one knew where she was. She smoked two more cigarettes and after a lot of hugging from me she left out the back door and my then-boyfriend tried to push it closed again. A part of the wooden molding fractured off so we stuffed a towel in it to keep the spiders out.

TWO JACKSONS.

In the parking lot outside of Star Seeds my then-boyfriend hugged me and told me he knew two Jacksons. One was in the physical world that he wanted to punch. The other, he said, was inside my head that he could never reach.

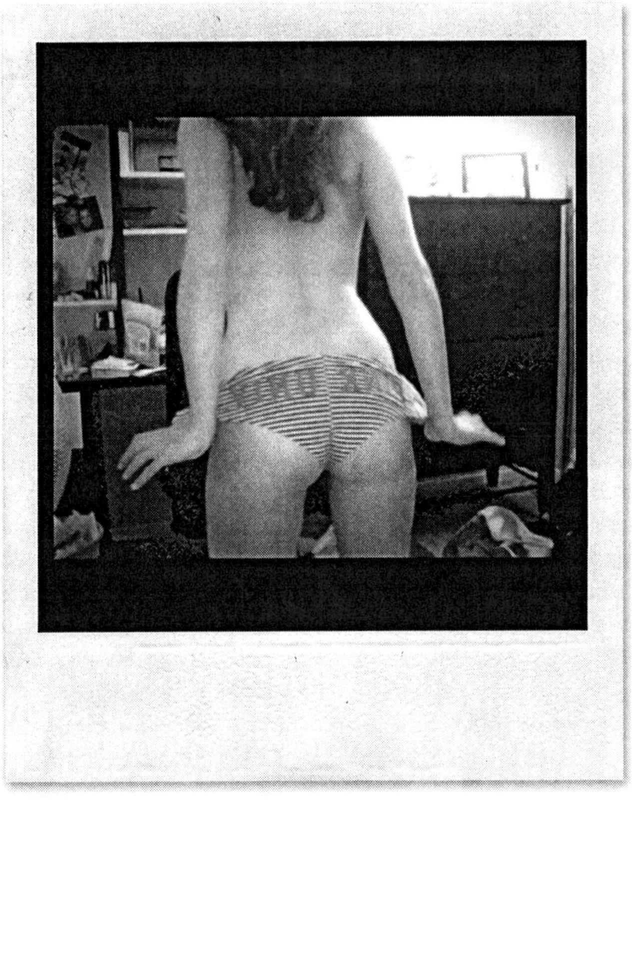

DRIVE.

While I was sitting on the green couch in our living room my roommate came home from work. It was early in the morning and I had no intention of going anywhere. "What're you doing today?" she asked. I shrugged. We stood in the small hallway between our bedrooms and my roommate tried to show me how to smoke out of a pipe my then-boyfriend gave to her for her birthday. "It's not working," I said. "I don't know how to do this." I tried once more but verbal instructions failed her and my roommate smoked demonstratively. Fifteen minutes later I realized it was working. "Let's go for a drive," she said. She drove a beat-up forest green Acura that she treated like a racecar. We rolled down the windows and turned the music up louder than was comfortable. My roommate sped down Highway 290 and headed east. The houses disappeared and the land stretched out with no mountains to cradle us. My world became a red View-Master 3D Viewer and all the images clicked by with the pull of an orange handle. Abandoned sheds, hazy horizons with as much likely to be over there as was over here—nothing except the occasional cow. My roommate pulled into a gas station and we got out. She started to fill up the tank. As always she wore her found sunglasses. She was the epitome of minimalist cool—a white men's V-neck and her prized designer jeans. They were always tight and low. She was my modern-day James Dean. I leaned against her car feeling the wind push up the skirt of my navy shirtdress. It was too hot that day to wear anything. Not wearing underwear was a good idea. I imagined what my then-boyfriend would say about it. Probably nothing. A big truck pulled up on the other side of the pump we were using. A man with tattoos and a shaved head came around the side to pump gas. He looked at us—staring and eating us with his eyes. My roommate finished pumping gas and we went inside. I bought a bag of puffy Cheetos and she bought some chocolate. We wandered back to the car and leaned against it, sharing my Cheetos. "Do you want to go to a park?" she asked. I nodded. After climbing back into the car she sped to a place overgrown with leafless trees and a large lake. Some kids were there with their parents, picnicking and enjoying the shade. We sat on a park bench for a few minutes before I asked to leave. We drove home and fell asleep on the couch watching *Twin Peaks*.

PRETENDING.

My then-boyfriend used to say there was something gross about strip clubs. "Strippers just *pretend* to like you," he said while smoking outside a strip club where we were buying a cheap dinner. "Who wants to pay someone to pretend to like you?"

ACCOUNTS RECEIVABLE.

Once signed on, a model logs into their chat room. People join in and watch the model's live camera feed for free. Sometimes models sit and stare, sometimes they converse with someone on the phone or with people in their chat room, and other times they are rarely in the free chat room at all. The idea is this: once in a free area people decide if they like a model or not. If they feel generous and want to share the experience they tip the model and they continue to perform in the free area. If visitors prefer a more private experience they can request a model perform for them in a private chat room where the paying visitor has access to the model's live camera feed—which costs money by the minute. A group of paying visitors can exclude all non-paying visitors and request a show just for their group. There is a bonus for those visitors who pay a membership fee and subscribe to a side offer that allows them to spy on the private shows of whatever model they choose. The visitor paying for the private show is never made aware that there is someone else watching—though the model is notified of every viewer. All money feeds directly into the website and a fraction is deposited in the model's account. From there checks get sent out to models.

BARFLY'S.

There was a bar known for its stiff, cheap drinks. I didn't drink—maybe once or twice and that was at the Girl Scout camp I worked at a few months before. My roommate and then-boyfriend had the night off together and we all decided to celebrate at Barfly's. To get into the bar you climbed up a narrow, shaky staircase. I learned one evening that the ever-present Austin breeze coupled with a flimsy skirt meant that plenty of people were guaranteed a surprise show. My roommate made a point of reminding me to wear underwear when we went out to Barfly's. Inside there were the requisite pool tables and cramped seating. The real draw was just past the side door where there was another rickety narrow staircase leading down and outside. The area was covered in Christmas lights, picnic tables surrounded by stadium seating. No one wanted to sit inside. We took our seats at the picnic tables and I drank three bottled hard ciders. My roommate bought me my first Long Island Iced Tea. My then-boyfriend let me try his Gin and Tonics. I don't remember what happened after that.

FAT.

Even when my ribs poked through my skin I couldn't suck it in any tighter. In middle school my mother noted the difference in the clothing I wore. I went from borrowing my brother's clothes—he is seven years older and much larger than me—to buying tight shirts and form-fitting jeans. "Suck in your stomach," she would say while patting and pushing my belly. "Suck in your stomach!" Later on my therapist lifted up my shirt. "Your stomach is fine," he said. I decided to stop trusting anyone else's opinion of my body.

TROLLS.

There were some people who visited the website to have a different kind of fun. They liked to tear down models, leave them disgusted or confused. These people were called trolls. They didn't often pay for anything but demanded a lot of time and attention. If a model didn't handle trolls correctly the model could be humiliated in front of potential tippers, or worse, trolls could overrun the chat room rendering it useless.

HUNGRY.

I came home for lunch. I shouldn't have been gone for more than half an hour but I took my time and sat at the kitchen table watching my then-boyfriend prepare the food. He offered and I accepted. He hated prep work, cooking, and dishes but for some reason on his day off the sun was shining and he had energy. He assembled messy quesadillas with black beans, oozing cheese, crisp peppers, and chicken he spiced and blackened on the stove. We devoured them and I watched him with hungry eyes. It wasn't the food I cared about. I could feel every part of me ache—my stomach, my chest, and between my legs. I didn't say anything when he served me but thanked him. I went back to work and felt comatose at my desk. When I got home he was out. Or asleep. Or otherwise unavailable.

THE LAST PUBLIC PERFORMANCE.

My roommate wrote a play about a family dealing with the suicide of their youngest boy. She asked me to play the part of the lesbian sister when her actual lesbian friend disappeared in her coke habit. All the actors, meaning her other available friends and myself, recorded voiceovers on my laptop. She propped it up on her underwear drawer in her closet. She had a plastic shoe holder hanging on the inside of the door that was always open and filled with designer shoes. We all stood, one at a time, in her closet and recorded our individual parts. She pieced them together so it could be played over the speaker system during the performance. There were parts that required me to show a lot of emotion. I used to be able to cry on cue but the only acting techniques I had left were to twist up my face and rub at my eyes. I couldn't cry and my heart was pounding in my chest on the stage. The girl playing my girlfriend forgot her cue to exit stage left so I bear hug tackled her and pulled her off—my then-boyfriend said it looked strange and I felt embarrassed. We performed once to a small packed house. After the end of our show there were a couple more plays but I escaped out the back and walked the gravel alley around to the front of the theatre. I sat on the metal bench and listened to someone shouting a monologue and people laughing. A guy named Sid in a black pork pie hat asked me if I had a light. I shook my head. His black-haired girlfriend sat next to me and asked if I was here to see a show. I told her I was just in one and they nodded. Sid was the best violin player in Austin according to his girlfriend. Sid bummed a light from a passing man. He offered me one and smoked through his at top speed. His girlfriend asked if I was interested in burlesque. I asked them if they had any connections. The girlfriend told me Sid was starting an experimental burlesque troupe that would do dark gothic shows. I listened and nodded. Sid offered me his number and I pretended to put it in my phone but their eager attitudes and wide eyes made me feel uncomfortable. The last show ended and people filed out of the theatre. Sid vanished and his girlfriend waved and followed. When my roommate and then-boyfriend came outside they asked where I went. I told them I had just been sitting on the bench the whole time.

TOES.

In an attempt to anchor the foot fetishists that breezed through my chat room I got pedicures regularly. It was expensive but I wound up loving the massage chairs and the feeling of the hot marbles pushing against the bottoms of my feet. I loved the soapy water soaking into my skin. The salon was wedged in the back corner of Highland Mall next to a forever-available empty store and a sports jersey shop. No one was ever there at the same time as me but the nail technicians were always too busy to get things done quickly. It was a one- to two-hour process. I didn't mind. I sat in the chair and listened to the *John Tesh Radio Show* or *Delilah*. I read tabloid magazines. The only time anyone spoke to me was to ask what color nail polish I wanted and how I wanted to pay. One time I fell asleep in the massage chair.

NORMA.

Norma had an invisible illness. Her file said she was taken in by the coworker with an encyclopedic knowledge of Austin social services and was given financial assistance with no limitations. That coworker quit and Norma was passed around the office as a client no one wanted. When she became my client I read in her file that she hadn't paid rent in almost a year. During our first meeting she told me I would never understand her illness. Her children stopped talking to her, she lost all she owned, and now she lived in a cramped apartment with as much of the furniture and memories she could keep from her old house and life. She cried every time we met. I discovered Norma wanted me to feel badly for her and she wanted me to cry with her. But I never cried during our meetings. I cried in my car after them.

ERIC.

Eric asked me if I wanted to know his deepest, darkest fantasy. The answer is always yes. He then said, "I heard you say you were on your period. I have always wanted to pull a tampon out of a girl during her heaviest flow. With my teeth." I was not menstruating. That was an excuse not to do anything too messy. I was trying to fight a stomach virus that was passed around my office. I did not have a lot of time between pausing my camera and vomiting in the trashcan underneath my desk. After wiping my mouth on a rag I resumed the live feed. "What's wrong?" Eric asked. "Was that too much?" I shook my head. "Not at all. I have always wanted someone to do that!" I said. That night he paid me $15 to eat a banana on camera. I threw that up too.

SOMETHING FUNNY.

My then-boyfriend was always hit on by the baristas in the front of the house. The owner hired very Austin-looking girls. They never wore bras, had gorgeous tanned skin, and effortless just-fucked hair. My then-boyfriend told me he hated the attention but they were the only stories he told me about work. I walked to Cherrywood to buy a bottled Coke. One of the baristas, Shannon, told me she had been waiting to share something funny with me. I pored over the pastry case thinking about the cinnamon rolls. She told me she had a fling with another cook in the kitchen and right before she orgasmed she called him by my then-boyfriend's name. I asked for a cinnamon roll and left.

UNDERCOVER STYLE.

The sandy blonde girl who worked behind the counter was always bored. She chewed gum loudly, kept her eyes on the computer screen, and never said hello. My then-boyfriend was obnoxious and always in tow. She laughed at his jokes and would smile at me after I handed her my credit card. The dressing room was a moldy beige box with a full-length mirror leaned against the wall. The curtain never closed all the way and you had to be sure there wasn't a camera hidden somewhere. My then-boyfriend would chuck the more obscene and neon pieces through the curtain, which I left untouched on the floor. The light in the fitting area was a single uncovered bulb above the mirror. I spent a lot of time looking in that mirror and poking at my hips or doing a breast lift with my hands. "Are you done yet?" my then-boyfriend asked. "What do you think of this?" I asked, pulling the curtain open. No one else was in the store. "I like it. I bet you could make a lot of money with that," he said.

SNOW DAY.

It was winter and I left the house early enough to let my car warm up. On the way to work it started to snow. When I arrived at work everyone in the office was lined up at the window watching the snow float onto the streets. "No work today," everyone joked. At around noon the man from Boston who was in charge of finances closed the office for a snow day. I went home and ate lunch with my then-boyfriend. We filmed each other outside and I edited it into a video postcard for my parents. We waved and laughed. The snow didn't stick.

CHRISTMAS.

There are times when someone is presented—in a split second—the Robert Frost poem about two roads. It seems, at the time, a harmless way of being honest with someone who asked a question. However, when the answer is revealed you will be called a prostitute, told you ruined Christmas, and forced to confess to the men of your family. When you refuse there will be consequences.

LUIS.

There were a good number of businessmen who frequented the website. They talked about their jobs ad nauseum. Luis was always traveling but prided himself on washboard abs. "There's no reason not to take care of yourself," he said. "I can tell you work really hard." He only ever wore a white bathrobe. He asked what I was willing to do, how much he had to pay, and told me I looked pretty. He loved his job buying pet products for a large chain. Luis liked negotiating, setting up the deal, acting on it, and tidying up with pleasantries. "Next week?" he asked. I told him I would be around.

ROD STEWART.

I sat on the couch next to my mother watching the Rod Stewart concert DVD she watched every year at Christmas. He sang old American songs and then some of his hits. I could barely breathe—convinced my mother would turn to my father and say with as much casual malice as she said to me, "Your daughter is a whore." I clenched my teeth while watching the high-definition picture of the audience singing along. Then I couldn't take it anymore. I went to the back of the house and listened to "You're In My Heart" one hundred and thirty-six times.

SUGA MAMA.

My then-boyfriend waited to pass out. He joked that he should quit his two jobs and let me take care of him. He said this curled up under the duvet while I was working and with sleepy eyes watched me dance until he crashed mid-sentence.

BALL AND CHAIN.

The first night I got blackout drunk I apparently told everyone that my then-boyfriend wouldn't have sex with me. My roommate assured me later that it was a passing comment but my then-boyfriend was furious. After dropping us off at home, my roommate sped off into the night avoiding our impending fight. My then-boyfriend got me into bed and left. He slammed the doors and walked down the street in the way he does when he's upset—hulked forward with his fists clenched. I went after him but could only make it to the end of the driveway where I sat on the gravel and cried. I was barefoot and in my underwear. He came back to yell at me before picking me up and putting me back to bed. He slept on the couch so he could make sure I wouldn't leave the house again.

GUILT.

My mother started to cry. "You have absolutely ruined Christmas," she hissed. I started to cry too. Since birth I had been conditioned to feel my stomach drop out and my skin flush hot with a disappointed word from my mother or a look from my father. They had me trained to sweat guilt. "You know why you're crying, don't you?" she asked. "Because you know what you've done is wrong. It's wrong and you feel bad about it. But you have to deal with the consequences. You are going to tell your father and your brother. We raised you better than this." I sobbed harder. In the following months I refused to take my mother's phone calls and my older brother panicked. He tried to mend our broken bridge but I held out as long as I could. I was a whore. I ruined Christmas. Most confusingly, I didn't feel what I did was wrong. That wasn't why I cried.

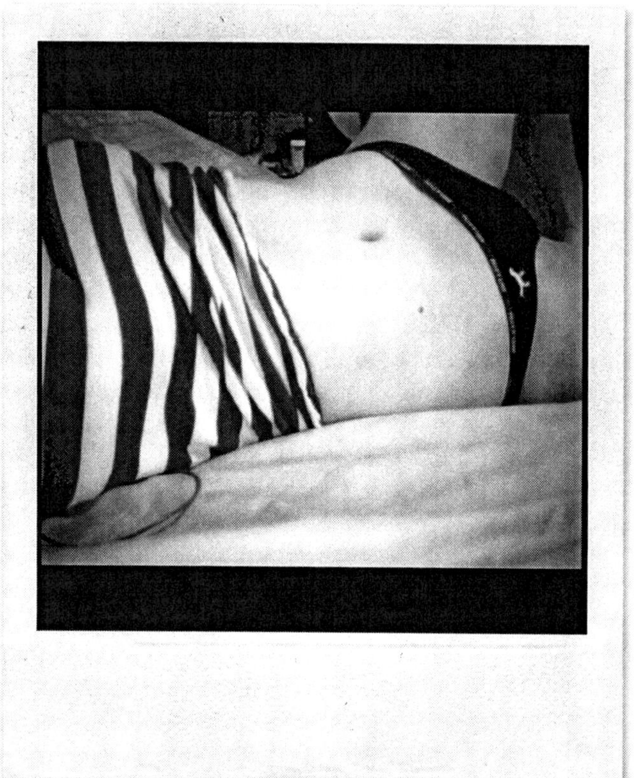

JC.

He looked a lot like Santa. JC had a hole in his neck but you could never tell with the long scraggly beard covering it. Sometimes he would lift it up and flash it at me with a big hearty laugh. I sat down at his kitchen table that was littered with candy wrappers. "This stuff's not good for you and your diabetes," I would remind him. "Don't give a shit," he'd mutter into a tin canister of caramels. My coworker would sometimes visit with me but JC was racist and she would get upset. "Fucking Mexicans!" he would yell with no provocation or any previous conversation about Mexicans. "I'm Mexican," my coworker would say. "Well that's too bad for you!" he would yell. She shook her head. I asked her about it once and she said she couldn't let every client's weird mental problems get to her or she'd turn out to be exactly like them. One time while trying to find one of JC's medicine bottles I found a soiled copy of *The Ethical Slut* by Dossie Easton. I first encountered it in one of my sexuality courses I took at Arizona State and I wondered why JC would even have a copy. I imagined him pushing through a bookstore to find something so salaciously titled to bring it home and find it was less *Penthouse* and more personal theory. I spent a lot of time filling out applications for permanent affordable housing with him. He hated applications. "Bunch of bureaucratic horseshit!" he'd yell. Whenever they would ask if he'd been convicted of a felony he would write, "Haven't been caught yet!" And with other questions he would write, "None of your goddamned business!" So I started filling out the applications for him and bringing them over for him to review and sign. He smiled like he taught me a great lesson. Another time I sat down at his kitchen table to find him slurping coffee and looking at an enlarged map. "I'm going fishing in Alaska," he said to me. "My brother's a sheriff out there in Wasilla—where that Sarah Palin's from? My brother is a cop there." I nodded. We were supposed to ask him how he was going to get there, with what money, and if he thought he could survive the weather with all the ailments he had. But I just wanted to give him some of my money and tell him to go. I envied his freedom. He arrived in Austin mysteriously. Someone found him asleep on a downtown bench. He told everyone someone stole his pick-up truck and he drove it from Missouri. With nothing left to his name he got set up with our program and was living in one of our apartments for just a few months before he started to get the itch to leave. I smiled as he detailed all the things he was going to do when he got to the wilderness of Alaska. He warned me he was leaving but he did that most of the time he was my client. One morning he didn't show up for an appointment so I went to his apartment. It was as it always was, messy and dark but he wasn't there. He left a note thanking our group for the kindness and generosity. "See you never again!" he wrote.

JAD.

He was straight out of the seventies. He had a mess of dark hair on his head and a thick beard that pushed up an equally thick mustache. Jad always looked like he was about to say something. I wondered what he thought of me. Tight light denim jeans and a used up T-shirt—he worked manual labor in New Orleans, where he was from. He stood behind the counter at Cherrywood as the only straight guy at the front of the house. I wondered how many of the baristas he'd slept with. He was always just distant enough to never use or remember my name and just familiar enough for me to always assume he knew it. I tried to make eye contact as often as possible but he was just never interested in conversation, in me.

RENEE.

I rarely got anyone identifying as a woman in my chat room. It made it exciting when one showed up. Renee was a bleached blonde mother of four who just got out of a relationship with a much younger woman. She was exploring her sexuality and enjoyed younger girls. She offered to fly me out to Carson City, where she worked, and called me Flower. She said I was beautiful. I spent a lot of time talking to Renee about her kids, her ex-husband, and her ex-girlfriend. I tried to talk to her about my life too, but she wasn't interested. She later got bored when I wouldn't do anything anally on camera and stopped talking to me.

MOVING IN.

After returning home from visiting my family for Christmas, my then-boyfriend told me he might not be coming back from his visit with his own family in Portland. When I asked him why not my heart was beating so hard my body rocked forward with each pulse. He told me his ex-brother-in-law had kicked him out of the house. We had been dating for about six months when that happened. I had a panic attack at the idea of his absence. I started to shake even though I was living fine on my own for the duration of our vacations. I couldn't even visualize what it would be like to not see him again. "Move in with me," I said. When he flew back he got a key cut out of *Finding Nemo* metal and we rearranged the clothes on the red wooden shelf that acted as my dresser. It became our dresser. The floors became littered with empty cigarette packages, candy and straw wrappers, and his dirty socks. This was love.

THE INTERN.

Sometimes while my roommate was out front smoking my then-boyfriend would join her after he showered. He showered at least two times a day. After work and before bed. He refused to go to bed without showering, sometimes subjecting himself to the couch if he was too tired to make it to the bathroom. He showered after things made him feel dirty, especially if they made him feel oily or greasy. Those two words and the feelings they carried made him shake lightly or hit his face with his fist. But he loved wrapping a towel around his waist and standing out on our front porch with his hands on his hips. He would prop his foot on a chair and my roommate would laugh and say the neighborhood always had a good view. The intern that worked for the woman who lived behind us would stroll up the sidewalk from behind the house. She saw my roommate, waved and smiled, and then saw my then-boyfriend. The smile would fall off her face. The incidents were always the same, she was embarrassed and tried not to look. I imagined the wind blowing the towel open and my then-boyfriend grinning—the gap in his front teeth declaring him forever boyish.

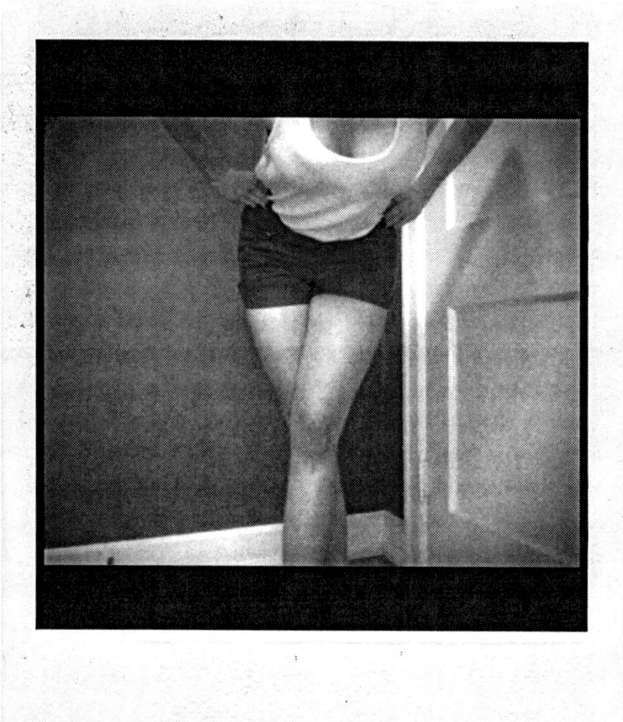

MLK DAY.

I was on a committee to plan a day of service for our volunteer organization to run and promote. We rented out a church community building and organized piles and piles of shoes and heavy coats. We arranged them on tables around a basketball court. Mobile Loaves and Fishes served food to a line that streamed out the side of the building and down a few blocks. I woke up that morning with a heavy head and a deep spike twisting in my stomach. I was assigned check-in first, which meant I sat at a table with a few other wide-eyed twentysomethings and wrote down details of ex-addicts and currently homeless people's lives. How did you fuck up? We don't judge, we said smiling. There were young people and old people. Healthy people and very frail people. Sick people and sick in the head people. I wrote down their names, their social security numbers, the reasons they thought they were homeless, how long they had been homeless, and what they wanted or needed. We gave them bracelets and like a factory farm pushed them into lines for services. I sat at another table and talked to people upset about their healthcare options and upset about all kinds of things. I realized soon enough they didn't want me to tell them names and numbers of people who could actually help them. They just wanted me to listen. I opened up the resource book we spent weeks compiling maybe ten times that day. I sat there with my hand underneath my chin. The entertainment committee had a local rap group perform. We smiled and filmed each other in matching gray T-shirts. We were hopeful and enduring amongst sad and lost people. I filmed a man who didn't speak English getting a haircut from a shy hairstylist. The man smiled at me, annoyed. I wondered if he was putting up with my camera because we got him a free haircut. There were foot doctors, dentists, and some other healthcare professionals around to administer free clinical care. People were thankful. We called it a success. I drove along IH 35 and couldn't remember how I got home.

COLLAGE.

My then-boyfriend worked nights during his bagel shift with a girl named Natalie. Because they shared the same sleep schedule they spent a lot of time together at work and then off work when my then-boyfriend didn't feel like sleeping. I got a text message from him saying they were going to go mud wrestle at a park by our house. I started crying. A few weeks later Natalie made my then-boyfriend a collage. On it were pictures she took from her camera phone printed out and pasted on a large poster board like a child's school project. She plucked old cigarette cartons out of the trash and fixed them onto the board. There were quotes, inside jokes they shared, and the words "I love you" scrawled on tiny parts—an attempt to bring to light feelings that my then-boyfriend knew were already there and mocked relentlessly. He refused to keep it, telling her he would just throw it away. She moved to New York at some point, and then followed us to Oregon. They still kept in touch. When we broke up in the spring a year or so later she asked if he would like her to move closer. He said no.

VIXEN.

I met Vixen once. She had fiery red hair and laughed loudly. She always had a comeback and oftentimes tilted her head into her neck and lifted her eyebrows to say it. The story was that Courtney sneaked into her house late at night and left before the sun rose. I saw him walking by our house a few times to confirm this but it was just a thing we laughed about. I saw Vixen's son more than I saw anyone else. Every day at the same time. My then-boyfriend called him Boondocks because he looked like Huey Freeman from the comic we loved. He was always walking his dog. Sometimes we would make eye contact as I drove by but we ignored each other like neighbors do nowadays. I didn't even know he was my actual neighbor for most of the time I lived in Austin. He was a lonely-looking coincidence.

LAWRENCE IN CHICAGO.

When I was living with three girls during college my first boyfriend and I broke up dramatically. I clung to our ended relationship and called his mother crying. We were supposed to get married and I was supposed to be with him forever. I became a soggy sobbing lump. Then a girl I used to work with who moved to Chicago started talking to me about her cute roommate. I thought it was a great idea to flirt with someone who was far away and learning about film. He played guitar and liked some of the same music as me. That was enough. I don't remember how we started talking but we spent a lot of time exchanging provocative pictures, sending dirty texts, and watching each other masturbate over the internet. We planned several times to meet in person. I never experienced such an overwhelming pressure in my chest I later identified as desire. I wanted him so badly—physically and emotionally. We would text constantly and shared our screenplays and short fiction with each other. His family was from Las Vegas—not a far drive from where I was going to school. When he went home for holiday break we planned to meet up but my first boyfriend and I got back together. I had my introductory trip and headfirst crash into a chasm of desire and conflict. I thought about what would happen if I just said goodbye and jumped in my car.

I told Lawrence we had to stop. But we didn't. Sometimes we would stop talking for weeks but if one of us got lonely, upset, or turned on there was always a text message and a picture to follow. We kept in constant contact while I was in Austin. I was inside an old apartment we finished cleaning out. I was supposed to wait for another client to come pick up a mattress and dresser from the bedroom. They were supposed to arrive with the truck at noon and the numbers on the stove read one o'clock. My coworker asked me to wait in the apartment while she went back to the office to meet with other clients. I sat on an old couch and texted back and forth with Lawrence. As our conversation turned down the route of unrequited lust I got so sick with pressure and desire I started to have a panic attack. I tried to masturbate on the couch but the anxiety and stress kept relief just out of reach. I stood out on the back porch with the old client's moldy and decaying belongings stacked around me. Rain fell hard but nothing cooled me off. The new clients came and I helped them move the dresser and mattress into a truck and waved goodbye. I was dizzy all day with numb hands and pins in my feet. I went home and went to bed. My hands tried to work out my feelings but nothing happened. We stopped sharing writing, emotional feelings, and pictures. I still so wanted his attention but it was always the same letters and punctuation. "He treats you badly. He doesn't deserve you. Come see me." I knew things were different after we stopped talking and both of us began new relationships. I didn't bother to reach out to him anymore. He didn't contact me either.

SOAPY.

I saw a model sit in a tub surrounded by empty glass bottles of liquor and some tipped-over pill bottles. She slurred her words and slid around in the soapy water. The people in the chat room said nasty things, some were concerned for her safety as she mumbled and moved around, soaked and sloth-like. I watched her for a half hour before she passed out with the camera on. People started logging out and I had to go to work so I closed my laptop. I wanted to check on her a few days later but I forgot who she was.

TAXIDERMY.

It was Jackson's birthday so my roommate wanted my then-boyfriend and I to accompany her on a birthday present hunt. We wound up at a taxidermy shop that looked like an old wooden cabin and was next to an old tin shed. The shop displayed large hides strung up and flapping in the wind, caked in the sun. I never knew what the shed was, even having driven by it several times, until that day. We got lost in the aisles of tiny chipmunks driving plastic cars with goggles on their heads to mismatched reptilemammals. My roommate wound up buying Jackson two animals one of which, a raccoon, stayed with us longer than I would have liked. It was adorned with my grandmother's old costume jewelry, a fur shawl, and made to hold a bottle of Bombay Sapphire. Jackson later buried it in his backyard with my grandmother's clip-on earrings still attached.

DOWNTOWN.

There were a handful of times my then-boyfriend asked me to drive him downtown. He didn't know how to drive. The word "downtown" elicits instant panic in me. I get lost on grids with well-placed signs and even with a calm electronic-voiced GPS I still make wrong turns. And then I panic. Then cry. But he still asked and I still tried. I would drive down the streets slowly, trying to make the one-way signs burn into my brain so I knew when to turn and when not to turn. Drunk people flowed like zombies from bar doors and it was then I began to panic. Everyone was driving like they knew where they were going. People passed me honking. "Are you freaking out?" he asked. "Yeah," I said. He sighed and said, "We can just go." I drove us home.

LIAM.

I became attached to Liam's username. There was a zero in place of an o. When he signed on he immediately came into my chat room and made jokes. "What's going on in here?" he said. "What are you all doing looking at my girlfriend?" There would be the occasional person who believed him and he exploded with sarcasm. Suddenly I would have a group of anonymous people spending their time together on the premise that they were going to see me naked. But we were a weird digital community. Liam never paid for any of the pictures I sent him or the video he got to see. Perks of being a favorite. We wound up meeting in person when I moved to Oregon. We sat in Pig Heaven, a restaurant in Vancouver, Washington. We ate baked beans and laughed about people paying for sex. "Is it weird?" I asked. "That we met on a porn site and now we're eating barbeque?" Liam and I hung out a few more times. Then he found a wife. It seemed like all he wanted to talk about was how to be a good significant other or what it looked like to be in a happy relationship. I stopped talking to him.

REVENGE.

I had to pick up my then-boyfriend from the airport. I showered, straightened my hair, pulled on a slinky black sleeveless dress, and struggled with the zipper for fifteen minutes. Cramming into a pair of blood red stilettos, I clomped out into the living room to ask my roommate for help. I found Jackson sitting by himself on the couch. My roommate was gone. "Can you zip this up for me?" I asked. He stood up and pulled the zipper all the way to the back of my neck. "You look really nice," he said. I was so caught off guard I didn't respond. After picking up my then-boyfriend we went to eat and wound up back home. My roommate and Jackson were watching a movie. We exchanged hellos and my then-boyfriend and I hurried into our room. The next morning my roommate was smoking on our front porch. I sat at the table next to her and watched Moose eat weeds. "Jackson was wondering if he did that on purpose," my roommate said. "Did what on purpose?" I asked. "It just makes me wonder if he was only on you so you'd be loud and ruin the movie. Jackson was really annoyed." I apologized and went back inside the house.

RUNNING.

My then-boyfriend found a free application for his smartphone. It played music and at the correct time would notify the listener to run or walk for certain amounts of time. The plan was to build up enough endurance to complete a 5k run. We would walk past Cherrywood, past the elementary school, past the houses teetering off steep hills, and past the median, and to the park my then-boyfriend affectionately dubbed the "Crack Park." We alternated running and walking. He would comment that I was too slow and that he thought I should try harder. I started to dread running with him because I could never run long enough or fast enough. I was always winded, out of breath, and one night I felt like I was dying. My then-boyfriend showered and went to bed. My lungs couldn't fill and even though my mouth was open, gasping for air, nothing came in. I hugged a pillow from our couch against my chest and felt it push forward but I was convinced I wasn't breathing. After calling my mother in a panic she urged me to shower and continue focusing on my breath. She suspected it was an exercise-induced asthma attack. I stumbled along the bathroom floor and felt the hours tick by like years. Everything was scary and then it just went away.

ACHIEVEMENT.

I helped Dorothy enroll in a free adult education course taught by volunteers. The curriculum was basic reading and math skills. During our weekly visits she would tell me about the tests she took with the three other students in her class. She was always worried she would fail a test. One time, on the bus, she received a phone call from her teacher to tell her how she did on a test she was nervous about. When Dorothy heard her score she screamed and fell out of her seat. The bus driver pulled the bus over and passengers helped her back to her seat. She cried in joy and embarrassment. Everyone laughed. She told me she loved school. Dorothy could read paperwork with my help and after a while she told me her teacher knew what the problem was. "I always had it in me. I knew how to read," she said. "I was just too afraid."

FRANK.

Frank was a silver Fabio look-alike. He held a lot of exotic fruit in his pictures. I imagined he walked everywhere barefoot and had a kitchen with an island of imported marble. "The other girls on this site have implants, fake tans, bleached-to-shit blonde hair. I don't like that," he said. He spent a lot of time in his messages detailing what my body looked like and how it was different from the other models. Sometimes he analyzed every pixel. "Do you know how to drive?" he asked. I told him yes. He asked if I would be interested in taking a trip with him to Cuba. He wanted me to be his chauffeur. "What side of the road do they drive on?" I asked. He asked if I would like some more pictures of him. I said what I always said: "Yes, please." A bolded line appeared in my inbox with a paper-clipped attachment. The pictures normally did not include faces. This was how I knew Frank was not a part of the digital age. His photographs were travel photos of his trips to remote mountains and lavish resorts. They were not photos of detached hands and penises. Frank sent a picture of himself standing beside Stevie Wonder. "He has gained a lot of weight since then," Frank said. I asked if Frank still looked the same and he said, "Of course. I treat my body like a temple. I can see that you do too." I said of course while pushing my large Styrofoam cup out of view.

EMPATHY.

I woke up, washed my face, put on my business casual, and strapped on shoes. Walking out to my car I felt the November wind hitting my face and hands. I tried to walk faster and as I approached I saw my driver's side window was smashed in. The glass of the window, now reflecting shiny turquoise, lay all over the seat and the backseat of my car. I stood in the middle of the road looking at it. The stereo was pried out and cords were frayed and exposed. I reached out and pushed in some of the glass that clung to the door. It cracked and fell onto the driver's seat noiselessly. Just then a couple of older women were speed walking by with pink visors and a golden retriever. "Oh!" one of them gasped. "Did someone break into your car?" I looked over my shoulder and watched them speed walk past. They didn't stop. "What a shame!" one of them called out as they moved down the road, pumping their arms back and forth. I went back inside and called my office to let them know I'd be late.

FREE.

On the website Craigslist there is a section where people can list things they are willing to give away. Oftentimes there are listings that advertise things people have left out on their driveways or front porches—just free for the taking. I would come home to find my then-boyfriend and roommate passed out on the couches with our living room covered in acquired items. One time I came home to the sun setting. The lawn was covered in a freshly claimed wicker lawn set. My roommate and then-boyfriend wrapped Christmas lights all around it and were sitting on the furniture smoking when I pulled up. The grass wrapped the furniture and lights in its overgrown arms and Moose hid inside the wicker table that used to have a piece of glass on top. He was the centerpiece to the free lit-up wonderland.

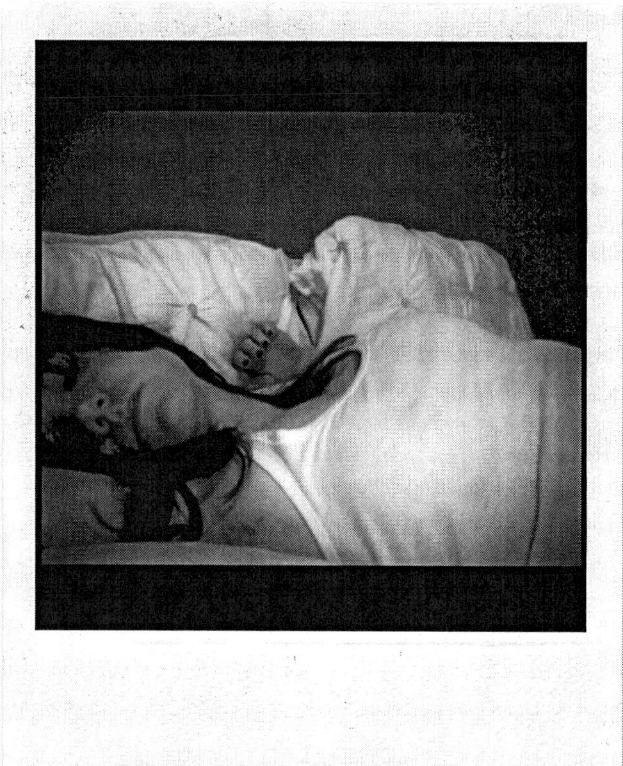

CHARITY CASE.

Norma was on the waiting list for St. George's Court for what seemed like forever. She passed on an opportunity to move in because she didn't like the apartments or she missed important paperwork—I'm not sure which but I do remember her behavior was grating on my supervisor and my coworkers. Norma was running close to getting kicked out of our program. My supervisor wanted her to make more of an effort to find a place to live but as usual with Norma she spent most of her time crying and then pleading for more time. I didn't think it was very fair to kick her out just because waiting lists for affordable senior apartments were on average two years. But, St. George's Court finally called and Norma got the okay to move in. On moving day we helped her with boxes of knick-knacks and dusty doilies. She cried because she couldn't get all of her furniture from her first house into the small apartment. For weeks after she moved in she would leave voicemails on my office machine wailing about how horrible St. George's Court was. She didn't get along with anyone and the apartment was just too small. I became angry when I heard the voicemails. I couldn't believe how ungrateful she was. My supervisor advised me not to return the messages. Still, I felt I was trying everything I could and giving her more than the other clients in our care and yet all she wanted to tell me was that it wasn't good enough.

NOTHING.

Once David sent me a message asking me why I was on the website. He said it made him sad to see girls like me doing things like this. I told him I needed to pay my rent. What I didn't tell him was that I liked being looked at and I liked being told I was pretty. I liked getting paid for those things and I liked getting attention. "When you're acting in my big Hollywood movie you won't need to do this anymore. We can live together and be really happy." I never responded when he said things like that. I didn't want to upset him. "What would I have to do to get you to stop doing this?" he asked. I told him he could pay my rent. "Okay. Then, will you stop doing this?" I told him I would stop until I needed to pay rent again. "Then you have to stop for the month. Don't do anything! Just live your life like you're supposed to." The next day I turned off my camera and wrote a check to the landlord.

PAINTING.

On Valentine's Day my then-boyfriend took me out to lunch at a Chinese buffet. We wound up at Jerry's Artarama afterwards. We wandered the aisles of overpriced art supplies and he reminisced about the days he used to tag sides of buildings and concrete walls with spray paint. We bought oil pastels and a pad of waxy paper. Sitting on the cold hardwood floor of our bedroom, we laid out the paper and began drawing and painting side by side. His painting turned into an abstract fish with a dark smeared background. I loved it so much I hung it up as soon as it was fixed and dry. Mine turned into an uninspired blonde girl that I later crumpled when no one was around.

BORN THIS WAY.

While at a family birthday party I was dancing on an ottoman. I must have been around six years old. I tried to recreate moves I saw on television and swayed my hips in circles. My uncle and father, beers in hand, noted how well I danced. Then my uncle said I would be a great stripper.

CAIRO.

One night my then-boyfriend and I went swimming with his closest friend and fellow cook, Cairo. We met him at his apartment that was covered in small bugs marching along the white walls and dusty baseball hats lining the kitchen counter. We walked down the street to an adjacent apartment complex and threw ourselves into the pool. As my then-boyfriend got out to smoke, Cairo and I held onto the side and kicked our legs out behind us. He asked me if I had any available friends. I told him they were all gay or taken—which was weirdly how it was. He asked me where he could meet a nice girl like me and I told him I wasn't sure. He started to swim a little closer and I pushed off the wall and tried to do a backstroke. We ended the night with burgers and because of the water stuck in my ear everyone's voices were distant and muffled.

BACK HOME IN ARIZONA.

I used a fake name and a fake location. I talked about things I didn't like as if I liked them. I told people I was a Scorpio. David asked if he could see me. I didn't respond. I received some more unsolicited money from him. He asked if he could see me. Then one night I received a long message telling me that he drove his truck off route. He went to Arizona and searched for me. He waited several nights in Phoenix. Why hadn't I responded? "We were supposed to meet," he said. I told him I didn't want any more of his money. I asked him to leave me alone.

PICTIONARY.

I was tired. None of the lingerie was ready to come out of the dryer and I hadn't eaten all day. I pulled out a notepad and drew. With the camera on the pad of paper, the people in the chat room guessed what it could be. I drew the president, a Flintstone car, a gun, and fruit. I got a good amount of tips. I got so many tips that I tried to recreate the situation a week later but the novelty wore off and no one stuck around.

METALLIC PINWHEELS.

Norma allowed me into her apartment. It was hot and muggy as usual. The rain was pouring down outside and her living room was filled with lace doilies, oversized furniture crammed side by side, and trinkets that reminded her of her estranged children and grandchildren. She was excited to show me something in a plastic bag. Her shaky hands pulled out a neon green-lined metallic pinwheel. She spun it around. I asked her where she got it and she told me she went to the dollar store. She told me about all the toys she wanted to buy but would have to wait for her next check. Before I left she grabbed my arm. "I put one in someone's yard. Do you want to see?" she asked. I said sure and after she piled on three heavy coats we walked outside of her apartment. "I can't be outside too long," she reminded me. We walked down the empty curvy sidewalks until a bright orange pinwheel came into view. The weeds and dying plants of the residents' yards looked even sadder in comparison to the pinwheel. We stood side by side and watched it spin. "I think he likes me," Norma said, referring to the man whose yard she stuck the decoration in. I smiled because it was the first time Norma did not cry during our meeting.

RAY.

I wanted to take professional-looking pictures. People paid more money when they saw you could cross over from amateur to professional. They liked to pretend they were talent agents. You could model! You could act! Ray was a photographer who also refereed roller derby. He had a tattoo on his arm of a roller skate with wings. On his other arm there was a tattoo of a nude alien woman. After getting in touch we set up a session. Before that we went on a date. My then-boyfriend and I were not speaking and I was convinced we were on the verge of breaking up. I numbed myself to the idea and decided Ray's attention was going to be good for me. We went to a bar where he invited all of his friends. They excitedly chatted with me about everything and anything and we wound up back at his house. I looked at pictures he took from trips around the world and I listened to the more dangerous and exciting stories he had behind the photographs. He started to get nervous. I asked him to take me home. We didn't talk for a while and my then-boyfriend and I didn't break up. Ray remembered the photo session we were supposed to have. I told him a good time for me and he told me to make sure I didn't wear any clothing for at least an hour before—to remove any marks or lines. His equipment was bulky and he spent a lot of time screwing and unscrewing things. My then-boyfriend was passed out in the bedroom we shared. There was a large umbrella attached to his flash that made it feel like that moment in movies when a nuclear bomb drops and everything is silent before an enormous flash of light. It's hard to keep your eyes open. Suck it in, pop it out, tilt the head back, and stop doing that with your face! Look over here. That's it. He wanted a Maxim-style shoot but I wasn't a Maxim-style girl. The photographs made some money but I broke the CD they came on and deleted whatever was left.

TIRED.

I started to fall into a familiar pattern. When my alarm went off I shut it off and just never woke back up. Hours and hours would go by and the days I meant to be productive just slipped into weeks ago. When my then-boyfriend would walk into our bedroom he would ask if I did anything that day. Sometimes I would lie and say I had. "You should work some," he would suggest. "It'll make you feel better." I could always sleep more.

ABOVE THE SINK.

I came home from work once and went into the kitchen. My roommate cleaned that day and everything was spotless. Hanging above the sink mounted to the blue tiled wall was the acoustic guitar Jackson smashed on our front porch. My roommate reassembled the pieces into a sculpture and hung it up above our sink.

CHAOS IN TEJAS.

Some childhood friends of my then-boyfriend were visiting from Portland for a big punk weeklong festival thing. My roommate consented to letting them park on our couch and I pretended to be asleep the night they arrived. I was terrified of them. My then-boyfriend told me it was a big deal to meet his friends. He felt that if they didn't like me it would be a deal breaker. I hid under the covers, pretending to be passed out and needing sleep for work the next day. Instead, I listened to them catch up. After awkward introductions the next evening we shuffled in and out of the house sharing the one bathroom with six people. There was Tony, the good-looking punk with long hair, ironic tattoos, and a bull's size septum ring. Always beside him was his gorgeous girlfriend, Anna. My then-boyfriend didn't speak to Anna much unless it was a joke about her being Asian which deeply embarrassed me. Tony's little brother, Mikey, arrived with a fresh diagonal cut across his face. He ran into a parked car in Portland on his bike just before the flight out. One of the days, while my then-boyfriend was working, I invited them to lunch at the co-op. I bought us all sushi with my food stamps. While Tony and Anna were poring over the organic and all-natural sodas, Mikey walked with me to the kombucha section. "So, uh, how did you two meet?" he asked. "I keep asking him but he tells me you two met doing crack under a bridge." I laughed because that was what my then-boyfriend told everyone—even his parents. "We met on the internet," I said. "I knew it!" Mikey yelled. "Like on Craigslist?" he asked. "No, like a dating website," I said. I tried to spend more time with them but our schedules were not in line. They wound up going to a water park with my then-boyfriend, leaving Mikey at our house because he couldn't swim with his face gash. I offered to spend time with him but my words were awkward and fumbled. We both muttered pleasantries and no-thank-yous before I left the house with nowhere to go. They flew back to Portland without a pair of Anna's jeans that I still wear.

POISED.

There are things that I will not do: snort cocaine, throw up after eating, and purposely cut myself. It is not that I am not capable of doing these things. In fact, I have thought about them for most of my life. The reason is because I know I will snort myself into an early death in a deteriorating hotel room, become a fraction of myself with rotting teeth, or I will push the knife deep enough to reach in and pull my insides out. There is not a question of theatrics. I am forever poised on the razor's edge.

A SERIES OF SHOTS.

First a kiss. White ribbed tights with holes on the toes. Dancing on hardwood floors. A lot of giggles. My then-boyfriend getting lost in the duvet cover that was donated to us from Crate & Barrel. My then-boyfriend playing harmonica and making family-unfriendly jokes. Some more giggles. A bit of music. I deleted all of it.

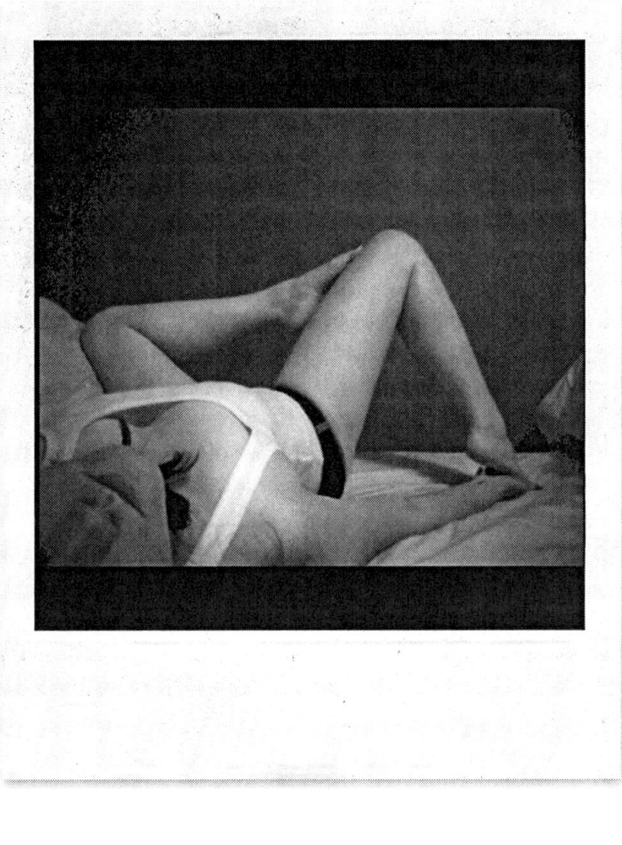

MY BULLY.

In middle school I spent hours in my room writing notes to myself and leaving them behind my dresser, my mirrors, on the walls behind my bed, and folded up in my pockets. I was split. Part of me raced to beat myself down. Horrible, nasty notes hung around me but were hidden to everyone else. I cried at my own emotional terrorism. I knew what sudden excitement was, the fleeting thrill of joy, and I had experienced slow-burning anticipation. But I didn't know what happiness was. "I just want you to be happy," my mother said to me every so often. When I thought about it, I didn't know what it was like to see my mother happy either. We mirrored each other's vacant stares. All her problems became my problems yet we were surprised each time. Even though I shared my brain and soul with her she had always been emotionally distant and someone I knew very little about. At twenty-two I didn't know more than a few perfunctory facts about her. The rest was an embarrassingly gaping hole—a story I would never know. She would never tell me if she ever tried to kill herself, or thought about killing herself. I wouldn't know if these thoughts were organically mine or genetically bloomed. She wouldn't even admit to smoking pot in her youth but my father told me they did. I wondered what other secrets she had that would eventually become my own. One night I excused myself from the living room where my roommate and my then-boyfriend were ribbing each other and grabbed my towel from behind our bedroom door. I went into the shower and turned it on. I pulled the curtain closed behind me and stood there, naked. That's when I began to shake. I squatted down and held my knees, feeling the water push my hair heavy down my back and around my face. The quieter I tried to weep, the harder it was to breathe. The boneyard of old razors my roommate and I used for shaving sat on the ledge of a window just above my head. I touched the tile and scum-filled grout above me. I inched my fingers over the edge and cried harder. Most of my suicidal thoughts before this were behind the wheel of a vehicle. I didn't tell anyone about them because I had been through enough therapy and attended plenty of suicide-prevention trainings to know once you admitted to it you were on the radar. Like every other time this happened there was suddenly two of me. I pushed myself against the sweaty tiled wall like a bully. I pleaded up at myself for my life. I knew I never went halfway with anything and this would be no different. I would be gone. I thought about my clients. Some had grown up in poverty and continued to live in constant struggle and forever worry. I wondered if they knew what it was like to have a different set of circumstances. I tried to pull my hand down from the ledge but my bully pushed my fingers along the edge of a pink disposable and I felt the pain and warmth of a new cut. My blood slid down the wall and I stuck my finger in my mouth. I could feel my heart beating against my tongue. If the infinite sadness I saw in my genetics was any indication I knew this would not be the last time I bullied myself to end it. I pushed my hands down where the water began to pool around the clogged drain. As the water rose I thought about lying down. I was dizzy. It was just one of me then. I was flushed and sweating. I felt the shower go cold and a surge of excitement pricked my arm hair up. I was awake and I was still alive. I started shivering for a different reason as my body temperature dropped. I wobbled out of the shower to my towel. I combed through my dirty hair with my fingers, went into the bedroom, and climbed into bed. I spent the rest of the night counting out my breath. I wondered when and where my bully would catch up to me and bleed me out.

INCEST.

I didn't have too many trolls in my chat rooms. I was too new and didn't last long enough to gain any sort of reputation. Those that found me did it by chance. Some telltale signs of trolls were if they asked a model to put a shoe on their head or to put a Sharpie up their ass. These were things models did thinking they were genuine requests. I knew it was code for making us look like naïve do-anythings. I ignored what I could and banned the rest. One troll in particular would pretend he had a fetish that needed to be discussed. It was always the same. He wanted me to pretend to be his sister and engage in a series of humiliating scenarios that ended with him ejaculating in my shoe. He sent me hundreds of messages—all with the same exact scenario. He wanted my reaction but I was stone.

RAPE.

I was frustrated. My then-boyfriend and I hadn't slept together in three months and I just wanted to be touched by someone other than myself. I wanted him to tell me I was pretty. I took a shower and stood at the end of the bed. He was playing some handheld game. I told him how long it had been since the last time we slept together and how embarrassed I was to have kept tabs. He told me it was unfair to hound him about it. I told him I wasn't sure what to do—it felt like he just wasn't interested no matter what I did. He said my pushing him felt like he was getting raped. I gave up. I dried and cracked like neglected Vaseline.

HOT PINK SHORTS.

It was one of those rare Saturdays where my roommate and I enjoyed each other's company on our front porch. We watched our neighbors avoid us. It was hot, humid, and the sky was overcast. Moose wandered around in the overgrown grass and I listened to my roommate talk. For Christmas my dad bought me a pair of University of Arizona basketball sweatpants that I wore as often as possible. They fit an actual basketball player better than me but I liked them because they ate me up. My roommate lit up her fifth cigarette as a car pulled up in front of our house. It took me a moment but I realized the person sitting inside was Natalie. "Who the fuck does she think she is?" my roommate asked when she realized the same thing. I stayed quiet. Natalie got out of the car. She started up the walkway as it began to rain. She stood on the concrete sidewalk leading up to our front porch but didn't come any closer. She yelled through the sound of the rain crashing down, asking if my then-boyfriend was home. We sat dry underneath the covering and stared at her. My roommate blew smoke into the air. "No," she said. The truth was that he was sleeping. I figured she knew that. "Well, he has a pair of my shorts," she said. We didn't take our eyes off her. "That's too bad. He's not here," my roommate said. "Oh. Well, he said he has them? Can I come inside and look?" Natalie asked. "No," my roommate said. The rain made her look like a shivering lapdog, her bony knees wobbled. Her eye makeup was beginning to run down her face and all I wanted was for her to come closer. I was simmering. She murmured something and got back into her car. I saw her texting and assumed she was trying to get my then-boyfriend to come outside. I found those shorts later on while doing our laundry. They were crumpled up in a plastic bag and stuffed into one of the pockets of his work shorts. He said she left them at work and he kept them to return to her but forgot. They were hot pink and barely a size small.

CHEESEBURGER.

I looked forward to going to Cherrywood sometimes, especially late in the evenings before they would close. It was a quiet time when the baristas were finishing up closing chores and the only people who were still around were a handful of Austin techies who were trying to finish projects before getting kicked out. I would order the Wife's Burger. It had a sweet wheat bun on it, a thick juicy burger piled on with stretchy cheese. I would ask them to put avocado, ketchup, onions, and lettuce on it. The French fries that came with the Wife's Burger were fresh, hand-cut, and lightly dusted with salt. I ate everything in one sitting and too fast. I must have eaten dozens of burgers during the time we lived by Cherrywood. I would accompany it with a bottled Coke and even though the process of eating it was messy and embarrassing I felt content for the briefest moment. I tried to eat the cheeseburgers alone or in corners with my back turned. The ritual was overwhelming. It tasted alive. After I would leave, never having said anything to anyone but my order and a 'thank you,' I would feel guilty and think about throwing up. I always thought about throwing up the cheeseburgers.

BLUFF'S LANDING.

Rick and Rita were a rocky couple. Rick was unemployed for a while during their time as our clients but he was one of the most active unemployed people I have ever seen in my life. He reminded me of my father—even when he had downtime he was working on something. Rita worked her whole life but was involved in an accident that affected her brain and emotions. She was put on all kinds of medication and financial assistance. My supervisor warned me that Rita would be a rollercoaster of a client. On some days she would cry to me about the inevitability of divorce between her and Rick. Some days she would float through the apartment and talk to me in song. Every day she would beg me to let her get a dog. I told her the apartment complex that donated units to our organization didn't allow pets and she would wail loudly with tears streaming down her cheeks. Seemingly overnight, an affordable elderly housing complex popped up and called to let us know they were accepting applicants. I applied for Rick and Rita and they were accepted. The problem was that it was in Round Rock, about twenty miles north of Austin—especially for someone like Rick who didn't have a vehicle. He growled and yelled about how inconvenient it would be. But Rita pouted, pleaded, and stared at him with puppy dog eyes—it embarrassed me to watch. She knew how to get him to say yes. I visited them after they moved in and Rick got Rita a tiny dog. The interiors of the apartments were beautiful. The kitchens had marble countertops, brand new carpet, and tiled floor. Rick and Rita had two bedrooms that already displayed Rita's unique clashing animal print style. On my last visit Rick showed me his new work uniform. Rita cried and thanked me. I told her it really wasn't necessary and that I was glad they had a home. I left them feeling like they were doing what they were supposed to—they were doing what they wanted.

FREE SWIM.

At certain times of the week Barton Creek had free swims and the creek would overflow with hairy girls and guitar-playing boys. Everyone was high. At least that's what I heard. My then-boyfriend invited me a half-dozen times to go but I made excuses. The truth was that I had a panic attack at the thought of being in a bikini in the sun. I got sick thinking someone would see me. He stopped asking and started going with his coworkers. I was relieved.

STUCK.

My roommate fed me hard cider after hard cider and then dropped me off at the house. I was teetering drunk and walked into our bedroom. No one else was home and Moose was watching me as I looked around. There were cardboard boxes with our things piled in. My then-boyfriend and I were moving to Oregon together. I saw an empty box and climbed inside of it. I pulled the flaps down over me and curled up tight. It felt like a good idea until I realized how uncomfortable I was. Then I realized I was stuck. Feeling nauseous and dizzy I tried to push the box over but couldn't get it to wobble. I cried but nothing happened. I wound up passing out inside of the box. I guess I hoped my then-boyfriend would come home to find me. But neither my roommate nor my then-boyfriend came home that night. In the morning I was sick and had to pee. I threw myself out of the box and felt my muscles stretch out with a painful freedom. When I finished in the bathroom I didn't want to go back to the bedroom so I sat on the couch and waited for someone to come home.

POST-ITS.

One client had such awful memory his entire apartment was covered in yellow post-its with blue pen drawings and reminders on them. The door had one that said, "Lock the door!" his computer had one that said, "Don't give out your social security number!" and he had three on his kitchen table reminding him to do the dishes, throw away his trash, and to make sure the lights were turned off when he left. He had a large whiteboard calendar fixed to the back of his front door and another one next to his bed. He wrote everything down and did so immediately after it was decided. An accident during surgery granted him an income from the hospital for the rest of his life but he was always frustrated. He was a client of ours because he couldn't remember where large sums of his money would go. I sat down with him and looked at his checking account register online. There were numerous charges to dating websites that totaled to more than $200 in monthly expenses. I asked him if he was dating. He told me he was active in his temple trying to meet women but didn't remember signing up for any dating sites. We canceled his memberships and he told me, now that he thought about it, it was possible he signed up for those dating site memberships. He said he was very lonely but didn't blame women for not being interested in him. He wasn't sure if he could remember them and if he could he wasn't sure they'd put up with his forgetting everything else.

DO YOU STILL?

Do you still want me to take you to the corner store? Do you still want cigarettes? Do you still want to borrow my food stamps? Do you still want to get high? Do you still want a milkshake? Do you still want me to bring you lunch? What do you want?

ACKNOWLEDGEMENTS.

I want to share my eternal gratitude to all those who have cared for me in the creation and development of this book. To those who dealt with things like late night crying and sloppy nachos. In particular I want to thank Nicole Loran, Todd O'Boyle, Justin Whiteaker, Micah Traylor, David Celis, Tonia Smith, Megan Jones, Jaclyn Spellman, and Diana Luu.

Several have been heroically present as this project exploded from a small essay to a book. I would like to thank Tiffany Lee Brown, Amy Lauren Botula, Jennifer Mann, Kevin Sampsell, and Katie Paschall for their feedback.

Thank you Greg Gerding and University of Hell Press for taking me on and creating beautiful and challenging things. Thanks Eirean Bradley for being a badass.

I want to send a very special thank you to the Independent Publishing Resource Center in Portland, Oregon and to the wonderful staff and volunteers who have only ever encouraged me and provided me with the materials to dream. Justin Hocking, A.M. O'Malley, and Michael D'Alessandro—I couldn't be any more thankful for the support you have given me even if I tried really hard.

xoxo,
Lindsey

ABOUT THE AUTHOR.

Lindsey Kugler was born and raised in Tucson, Arizona. She was a dedicated performer in high school with mock trial, policy debate, and speech events. She is a college dropout who has never cared about school. She has worked and currently works exclusively for nonprofits—except for a couple-month stint as an office assistant where she made more money than she ever had before and probably ever will again. In the spring of 2012 she graduated from Portland, Oregon's Independent Publishing Resource Center certificate program in self-publishing. She lives in Portland, Oregon.

HERE. is her first book.

Available from University of Hell Press:

by Eirean Bradley
the I in team

by Calvero
someday i'm going to marry Katy Perry

by Brian Ellis
American Dust Revisited

by Greg Gerding
The Burning Album of Lame
Venue Voyeurisms: Bars of San Diego
Loser Makes Good: Selected Poems 1994
Piss Artist: Selected Poems 1995-1999
The Idiot Parade: Selected Poems 2000-2005

by Lindsey Kugler
HERE.

by Johnny No Bueno
We Were Warriors

by Stephen M. Park
High & Dry

HELL PRESS
UNIVERSITY OF HELL PRESS

CPSIA information can be obtained at www.ICGtesting.com
Printed in the USA
BVOW04s1532240913

331560BV00002BA/7/P

9 781938 753039